WHY DOES
DEMOCRACY
MATTER?

Jessica Pegis

Crabtree Publishing Company
www.crabtreebooks.com

CITIZENSHIP IN ACTION

Author: Jessica Pegis

Series research and development: Reagan Miller

Editors: Petrice Custance and Reagan Miller

Proofreader: Janine Deschenes

Design and photo research: Margaret Amy Salter

Prepress technician: Margaret Amy Salter

Print and production coordinator: Katherine Berti

Photographs

Shutterstock.com: Kenneth Sponsler: cover (background-left); arindambanerjee: page 5; Krista Kennell: page 7 (top left); Jose Gil: page 7 (bottom); muratart: page 8; Anton_Ivanov: page 10 (right); Erika J Mitchell: page 18
All other images from Shutterstock

Library and Archives Canada Cataloguing in Publication

Pegis, Jessica, author
        Why does democracy matter? / Jessica Pegis.

(Citizenship in action)
Includes index.
Issued in print and electronic formats.
ISBN 978-0-7787-2597-8 (hardback).--
ISBN 978-0-7787-2603-6 (paperback).--ISBN 978-1-4271-1774-8 (html)

        1. Democracy--Juvenile literature. 2. Equality--Juvenile literature.
I. Title.

JC423.P338 2016   j321.8   C2016-904140-9
                                                                    C2016-904141-7

Library of Congress Cataloging-in-Publication Data

CIP available at the Library of Congress

Crabtree Publishing Company

www.crabtreebooks.com   1-800-387-7650

Printed in Canada/082016/TL20160715

Published in Canada
Crabtree Publishing
616 Welland Ave.
St. Catharines, Ontario
L2M 5V6

Published in the United States
Crabtree Publishing
PMB 59051
350 Fifth Avenue, 59th Floor
New York, New York 10118

Published in the United Kingdom
Crabtree Publishing
Maritime House
Basin Road North, Hove
BN41 1WR

Published in Australia
Crabtree Publishing
3 Charles Street
Coburg North
VIC 3058

What is in this book?

What is democracy? 4

Rights and laws 6

People power 8

Government keeps us safe 10

Three principles 12

More about equality 14

More about fairness 16

More about respect 18

Democracy depends on you 20

Learning more 22

Words to know 23

Index and About the author 24

What is democracy?

A **government** is a group of leaders who make **laws** and decisions for a country, province, state, or **community**. A community is a place where people live, work, and play.

Democracy is a form of government.
In a democracy, people **vote** to choose leaders.
They vote for leaders who stand for what they want
and believe. In a democracy, the government must
listen to the people.

Real Change Now
Changer ensemble
maintenant

Rights and laws

In a democracy, the government protects the **rights** of **citizens**. Citizens have the right to:

- ☑ Be treated fairly
- ☑ Vote for their leaders
- ☑ Follow their faith
- ☑ Speak out and share ideas
- ☑ Choose where to live

Governments make laws to keep people safe and to protect their rights. There are safety laws, such as wearing seat belts. There are free speech laws that allow everyone to speak out and share their ideas.

People power

Government leaders make many decisions that affect communities. They decide what to spend money on, such as fixing roads and building schools.

But how do leaders know that they are making the right choices? What happens if they make a choice the citizens do not like?

Government leaders must listen to citizens.

When a democratic government makes unpopular decisions, citizens vote for change. During an **election**, citizens can let the leaders know if they are unhappy by voting for new leaders.

"I promise to clean up all our parks!"

"I promise to build a new arena!"

Leaders have different ideas about what is best for the community.

Government keeps us safe

In a democracy, government works to make communities great places to live. The police are part of the government. They protect citizens. They work to stop people from breaking laws.

In a democracy, it is good to be different. Everyone is equal. That means no one is better than anyone else. No one can be left out. In a democracy, your right to be equal is protected by law.

Everyone is different.

More about fairness

In a democracy, there are rules and laws to make sure everyone is treated fairly. For example, in your classroom it may be a rule to raise your hand before you speak. This rule is fair because it gives everyone a chance to speak and be heard.

You can put fairness first by making sure everyone gets a turn and no one is left out.

Think About It

Once the day's lesson was over, Ms. Carey turned to her class and said:

"One day you will be able to vote in an election. But for now, how could you stand up for more equality, fairness, and respect in your life?"

How would you answer this question?

Learning more

Books

Hanson, Anders. *Land of the Free: The Kids' Book of Freedom*. Super Sandcastle, 2014.

Kopp, Megan. *Be the Change for the Environment.* Crabtree Publishing, 2015.

Peppas, Lynn. *Election Day.* Crabtree Publishing, 2011.

Web Sites

Check out this fun site for games and activities about democracy:
www.pbskids.org/democracy

Learn more about respect for others and how to stop bullying here:
http://pbskids.org/itsmylife/friends/bullies/

See how children around the world are standing up for democracy:
www.kidsgoglobal.net/

Words to Know

izens (SIT-i-senz) noun People who ⟩ong to a community

mmunity (CU-mu-ni-tee) noun A place ⟩ere people live, work, and play

mocracy (dih-MOK-ruh-se) noun ⟩orm of government in which people vote ⟩choose their leaders

ʒction (ih-LEK-shuhn) noun The process ⟩choosing a leader by voting

vernment (GUHV-ern-muhnt) noun ⟩jroup of people that run a country, ⟩vince, state, or community

ʋs (LAWZ) noun Rules made by ⟩vernment that people must follow

principles (PRIN-suh-puhls) noun Big ideas about the correct way to behave

right (RITE) noun Something you are allowed to have or do

vote (VOHT) verb Make a choice by marking a ballot or some other method such as raising your hand

A noun is a person, place, or thing.

A verb is an action word that tells you what someone or something does.

Index

citizens 6, 8, 9, 10, 13, 18

community 4, 8, 10, 18

democracy 5, 6, 9, 10, 12,
  13, 15, 16, 18, 20

election 9, 21

government 4, 5, 6, 7, 8, 9,
  10, 11, 13

laws 4, 7, 15, 16

rights 6, 7, 15

vote 5, 9, 21

About the author

Jessica Pegis is a writer and editor living in Toronto. She has written several books for teens and children in the areas of science, citizenship, and media awareness.